The Book of Benjamin

THE

BOOK

OF

BENJAMIN

Ben Robinson

Palimpsest Press
1171 Eastlawn Ave.
Windsor, Ontario, N8S 3J1
www.palimpsestpress.ca

Printed and bound in Canada
Cover design and book typography by Ellie Hastings
Edited by Jim Johnstone

Palimpsest Press would like to thank the Canada Council for the
Arts and the Ontario Arts Council for their support of our publishing
program. We also acknowledge the assistance of the Government of
Ontario through the Ontario Book Publishing Tax Credit.

LIBRARY AND ARCHIVES CANADA CATALOGUING IN PUBLICATION

TITLE: Book of Benjamin / Ben Robinson.
NAMES: Robinson, Ben (Poet), author.
DESCRIPTION: Essays.
IDENTIFIERS: Canadiana (print) 20230489001
        Canadiana (ebook) 20230489117

ISBN 9781990293603 (SOFTCOVER)
ISBN 9781990293610 (EPUB)
CLASSIFICATION: LCC PS8635.O24865 B66 2023 | DDC C814/.6—DC23

for Mom and Dad for giving me a name

for Emily

because we are words
and our meanings change

bpNichol

A MESSAGE DELIVERED BY BEN-
JAMIN ROBINSON AT OUR
EMERYVILLE CAMPUS. BEN ROB-
INSON-DRAWBRIDGE SPOKE
WITH MR. KUWEH, WHO SAYS
THE INDEFINITE DETENTION OF
REFUGEES ON THE ISLAND HAS
TARNISHED IT IN THE EYES OF
THE WORLD. ARCHAEOLOGIST
BEN ROBINSON, PICTURED,
EXPLORES THE STORY OF THE
VILLAGE FROM NORMAN TIMES
TO THE PRESENT DAY. THE
AGREEMENT, NEGOTIATED WITH
QUEEN VICTORIA'S REPRESENTA-
TIVE, WILLIAM BENJAMIN ROB-
INSON, PROMISED EACH FIRST
NATIONS CITIZEN AROUND $2 A
PERSON, WITH PROMISES TO
INCREASE THE ANNUITY AS THE
LAND WAS DEVELOPED AND
RESOURCES WERE USED. GARY
AND KATIE ARE CLOSE FRIENDS
WITH BURTON ALBION OWNER,
BEN ROBINSON, WHICH ALSO
SPARKED THE BREWERS BET. BY
CONTRAST, ASCARIDE RESISTS
THE ATTENTIONS OF FISHERMAN
BENJAMIN ROBINSON, WHO HAS
BEEN IN LOVE WITH HER SINCE
FIRST SEEING HER ON THE STAGE
IN MARSEILLE. BENJAMIN ROB-
INSON, AS RALPH RACKSTRAW,

The first time I met another person with my name was in junior kindergarten. This other Ben and I would attend the same elementary, middle and high school together. We were Ben B and Ben R.

It would not have been difficult to tell Ben B and me apart: my bright, primary blue glasses, his size he used to antagonize other kids.

Though I don't recall the details, I remember sitting on top of Ben B, punching down repeatedly into his torso – mad enough to fight but too afraid to actually hit him in the face.

Later, a third Ben – an identical twin – would arrive at our school.

ALSO ENJOYED A SUCCESSFUL DEBUT WITH EUGENE OPERA. WHERE ARE *BELOW DECK* STARS BEN ROBINSON, EDDIE LUCAS, KELLEY JOHNSON, AND AMY JOHNSON NOW? BEN ROBINSON IS NO LONGER WITH THE ORGANIZATION AND HAS STEPPED DOWN AS EDITOR-IN-CHIEF OF OBSERVER. IT TOOK NINE MONTHS NOT ONLY TO FIND BEN ROBINSON BUT TO CONVINCE HIM THE OBSERVER REALLY WAS AN ENVIRONMENT RIPE FOR CHANGE. BURTON ALBION AND MANCHESTER CITY ARE "CHALK AND CHEESE", SAYS BURTON CHAIRMAN BEN ROBINSON. BEN ROBINSON HELPED PERFORM CPR ON SUE AFTER SHE HAD A HEART ATTACK IN THE CAFE. "AFTER THE OLDER CHAP STARTED TO TIRE OF DOING CHEST COMPRESSIONS, BEN ROBINSON (WHO WORKS AT THE CHERIES) STEPPED IN AND WAS SUPERB." BEN ROBINSON TOLD SKY SPORTS NEWS, "IT IS VERY MUCH A CASE OF PINCHING OURSELVES AND THINKING IT IS ANOTHER GREAT OCCASION TO LOOK FORWARD TO." THE FOLLOWING BOLIVAR STUDENTS

My parents didn't know it when they named me but there have been at least two other Benjamins in my family.

My maternal grandfather's uncle was Benjamin Bootland. My grandfather tells me:

> My uncle Ben was my mother's older brother. He had a gruff demeanour but was very kind-hearted. He was good to my mother and always invited me and my oldest sister, Marilyn, to their family cottage at Peacock Point on Lake Erie. Ben probably didn't go to high school, but he was a very successful businessman. He had a trucking business and owned several rental properties in the City. He and his wife, Lorraine (a kind and beautiful woman), had four children and owned a home on King Street West just down from where the medical centre is now.

The second Benjamin was my paternal grandfather's grandfather, Benjamin Hodgins.

WERE RECENTLY NAMED TO ROCK-
HURST UNIVERSITY'S FALL 2018
DEAN'S LIST: OLIVIA COONS, MARY
HARRIS, BENJAMIN ROBINSON.
SECOND NINE WEEKS EFFORT
AWARDS - FOURTH GRADE: KYRA
ARMSTRONG, MADELYNN BACH,
SLOAN CLAUSSEN, BRAYDON
CORONA PANTOJA, ASHLEY HER-
NANDEZ, HAILEY HUGHES, JACK-
SON JONES, RYLIE MOORE, BEN
ROBINSON, AIDYNE SHANLEY,
CAMERON TERRY. STACY SOUTH-
WELL AND BEN ROBINSON LOST
THEIR DAUGHTER SOPHIE IN 2016
AFTER A BATTLE WITH A BRAIN
TUMOUR AND NOW THREE YEARS
ON THEY WANT TO HELP OTHER
FAMILIES GOING THROUGH THE
SAME THING. BENJAMIN ROBIN-
SON DRIVING WHILE IMPAIRED. IN
THE EARLY 1800S, DR. BENJAMIN
ROBINSON ACTUALLY BOARDED
PATIENTS AT HIS OWN HOME (NOW
THE BELDEN-HORNE HOUSE)
FOR TREATMENT. LOHUD WRES-
TLING SCOREBOARD: DUAL MEET
RESULTS FOR JAN. 15-17, 220:
BEN ROBINSON (YK) PIN MARK
CARACCIOLA (FL), 2:27. BEN ROB-
INSON III, MICHAEL BARNETT,
PHIL MALICOTE AND JEFF REED
WERE TAPPED BY FRALEY TO

The Book of Genesis describes Benjamin as the second son of Rachel and the last of the twelve sons of Jacob. While giving birth, Rachel realizes she will not survive, and in the final moments before her passing, she tells the midwife her son is to be named Ben-Oni – *son of my mourning* or *son of my sorrow*.

At some point after Rachel's passing, Jacob changes the child's name to Ben Yamin meaning *son of the right* or *son of the south* in reference to the region where Benjamin was born. The name can also be translated as *son of my days* in reference to Jacob's old age at the time of the birth.

SERVE ON THE BEREA PLANNING & ZONING COMMISSION. BEN ROBINSON KNEW HE HAD SOMETHING SPECIAL. BEN ROBINSON'S MUM, MARY, WHO STILL LIVES IN SUTTON HAS SAID THAT TONIGHT IS A PROUD MOMENT FOR HER AFTER SHE SPOTTED HER SON IN TODAY'S EDITION OF THE TELEGRAPH NEWSPAPER. JOINING KEN AND VADIM IN THE ENCHANTED FOREST ARE LEGENDARY DJ MR BENN "RU" ROBINSON, DJ HIPHOPPAPOTAMOUS, AAA BADBOY, AND WAGGLES. ARCHAEOLOGIST BEN ROBINSON EXPLORES THE FACTORS WHICH ALLOWED THE REMOTE COASTAL SETTLEMENT TO GROW: ITS ALMOST UNIQUE POSITION AS A SAFE HARBOUR, ITS HARDY VILLAGERS AND ITS STRATEGIC SPOT FOR EXPORTING DESIRABLE CORNISH GOODS. DR. EARL BENJAMIN-ROBINSON OF THE BACH GROUP IN NEW ORLEANS WILL CLOSE OUT THE CONFERENCE BY GIVING ATTENDEES ADVICE ON HOW THEY CAN APPLY ALL THE INFORMATION AND KNOWLEDGE THEY LEARNED THROUGHOUT THE DAY. "PERHAPS IF HE STAYS HERE LONG TERM AND WE GET THE BEST

The biblical translator Robert Alter writes, "This is the sole instance of competing names assigned respectively by the mother and father."

I can imagine Jacob would not have wanted his child's life defined by mourning and sorrow, but how long did he wait to change the name? Did Benjamin know?

OUT OF HIM, BEN ROBINSON CAN
GET THERE WITH HIM." DR
YOUNG TOLD BEN ROBIN-
SON-DRAWBRIDGE REQUESTS
WERE OFTEN DELAYED OR
DENIED BY THE BUREAUCRATS
TO MAKE THE REFUGEES SUFFER
AND THAT DEPRESSION AND
HOPELESSNESS HAD LED TO
SELF-HARM AND SUICIDE
ATTEMPTS BECOMING A DAILY
OCCURRENCE. BEN ROBINSON
ADDED, "THE VALUE PROPOSI-
TION OF THE MARKETPLACE IS
TO FIND THE BEST COMPLEMEN-
TARY SOLUTIONS AND TO PRE-IN-
TEGRATE THEM WITH OUR SOFT-
WARE." BEN ROBINSON HAS
FOCUSED ON HIS BUSINESS ON
LAND FOR SOME TIME, SO FANS
WERE HYPED TO SEE HIM IN THE
PHOTO. SRC BEDE'S CAMPUS
PRINCIPAL BEN ROBINSON SAID:
"THIS IS A GREAT OPPORTUNITY
FOR YOUNG FEMALE PLAYERS IN
THE TEES VALLEY AREA TO
ENTER A PROGRAMME WITH
RECOGNISED PATHWAYS TO THE
PROFESSIONAL GAME WHILST
CONTINUING THEIR EDUCATION
IN A DUAL-CAREER ETHOS."
DIRECTOR OF SALES AT ROBIN-
SONS BEN ROBINSON ADDS:

My family also has a name that is rarely spoken.

In between my younger brother and I, my sister Emily was stillborn. Growing up, my only connections to Emily were a tiny aluminum angel given to me by my parents, a family outing each year on her birthday to tend the children's garden at the church and the odd time my dad would bring a box of photos down from a shelf in his closet.

It has taken a child of my own to begin to understand that my mother was pregnant not twice, but three times, to consider what she might feel when someone asks how many children she has and what their names are.

"WE'RE CONTINUING TO DRIVE TROOPER AS THE BEER OF MUSIC, WITH A FOCUS ON CRAFT BEER BARS, PREMIUM OUTLETS, MUSIC VENUES, LIVE EVENTS AND MUSIC FESTIVALS." RAPID CITY RODEO FINAL RESULTS - STEER WRESTLING: 1. ELI LORD (STURGIS, S.D.) 4.7 SECONDS, $3,259 2. TY ERICKSON (HELENA, MONT.) 4.8, $2,916 3. (TIE) MYLES NEIGHBORS (BENTON, ARK.) AND HANK FILIPPINI (BATTLE MOUNTAIN, NEV.), 5.2, $2,402 EACH 5. BENJAMIN ROBINSON (HASTINGS, NEB.), 5.6, $1,887. IN ADDITION TO SHARING A HONGI WITH ROSS, SHE ALSO WORKED WITH AND KISSED BEN ROBINSON IN SEASON 1 OF BELOW DECK MED, BUT CAPTAIN LEE ROSBACH HAS NOTHING BUT GOOD THINGS TO SAY ABOUT HER. MARRIED ON JUNE 29, 2015, EARL AND MICHAEL BENJAMIN-ROBINSON WERE THE FIRST SAME SEX COUPLE TO LEGALLY MARRY IN THE STATE, STARTED THE FIRST BLACK GAY PRIDE CELEBRATION IN MISSISSIPPI IN 2004 AND OPENED ITS FIRST LGBT RESOURCE CENTER. THEIR WEDDING PHOTOGRAPHER, BENJA-

In a cupboard at my parents' house, there are eighteen photo albums – one for the decade between 1982-1992, then a new album every few years once my brother and I were born.

My sister passed away on April 30th, 1996. In the album spanning '95-'97, the chronology is messy. The photos move from my third birthday in December, to Christmas, then back to Halloween before jumping to my grandfather's birthday the next August.

There is one photo from May of '96 in the album. It's a nondescript shot of me, alone, age 3, seated at a desk, smiling in my grandparents' house. It is the only photo present from the first six months of 1996.

MIN ROBINSON, A PHOTOGRA-
PHER OF 15 YEARS, PLAYED A
MAJOR PART IN GETTING THEM
IN TO THE COMPETITION, PAUL
SAID. BURTON ALBION CHAIR-
MAN BEN ROBINSON SAID: "WE
HAVE BEEN DELIGHTED TO
WORK WITH OUR FRIENDS AT
PIRELLI AGAIN, NOT ONLY TO
PROVIDE EXTRA PARKING ON
SELECTED MATCH DAYS BUT TO
ALSO TO RAISE FUNDS FOR A
CHARITY THAT DOES INCREDI-
BLE WORK, FIGHTING ON BEHALF
OF BRAIN TUMOUR SUFFERERS."
OUR SCHOOL COMMITTEE REC-
OGNIZES BENJAMIN ROBINSON
FROM BURNCOAT HIGH SCHOOL
FOR HIS BRAVERY SAVING 8 PEO-
PLE FROM A HOUSE FIRE. THE
STRATEGY WORKED, AS FINN
WAS ABLE TO EARN A 6-3 DECI-
SION OVER YORKTOWN'S BEN
ROBINSON TO BECOME THE HUS-
KIES' FIRST SECTION I CHAMPION
IN MORE THAN A DECADE. BEN-
JAMIN ROBINSON IS KNOWN FOR
HIS "CHARMING LYRIC TENOR,"
"EMPHATIC CHARACTERIZA-
TIONS," "EASY VOCAL PRODUC-
TION AND...LUSCIOUS INSTRU-
MENT." BENJAMIN ROBINSON IS
A LIAR, MANIPULATOR, AND

One of my closest friends is also named Benjamin. People often ask if this is confusing for us, though we lived together for two years and never once confused the other for our self.

We are known collectively to our friends as "the Bens" or "Ben & Ben." Our wives specify "my Ben" and "your Ben." Sometimes we are "Ben" and "other Ben." I become Ben R again; he becomes Ben M.

Ben and I have played music together since we were teenagers. Ben does not perform under his first name or last name but his two middle names.

At shows, we often find ourselves meeting new people, sometimes both of us at the same time. We introduce ourselves as "Ben" and "also Ben" or "Ben" and "Ben as well."

CHEATER. HE WILL LURE YOU IN AND MAKE YOU BELIEVE YOU ARE THE ONLY ONE. I PROMISE YOU YOU AREN'T. OVER THE COURSE OF 3 BLOGS, DIRECTOR OF AGENCY SERVICES, BEN ROBINSON, WILL CONSIDER WHAT ESTATE AGENTS SHOULD BE THINKING ABOUT WHEN IT COMES TO IDENTIFYING AND MANAGING RISK, AND WHAT PROCESSES THEY CAN PUT IN PLACE TO ENSURE THEY COMPLY WITH THE AML REGULATIONS. BUOYED BY THE GOVERNMENT'S RECENT DEFEAT OVER A BILL TO EASE MEDICAL TRANSFERS FOR SICK REFUGEES, THOSE ON MANUS HAVE CALLED ON THE OPPOSITION TO SUPPORT NEW ZEALAND'S OFFER BEN ROBINSON-DRAWBRIDGE REPORTS. BURTON ALBION CHAIRMAN BEN ROBINSON HAS PAID TRIBUTE TO "A GREAT GENTLEMAN OF FOOTBALL" AFTER ENGLAND WORLD CUP-WINNING GOALKEEPER GORDON BANKS DIED, AGED 81. THE BARN ARTS PRODUCTION OF "THE BARBER OF SEVILLE," DIRECTED BY NICHOLAS TOCCI WITH PIANIST CLAIRE BLACK, FEATURES TENOR BENJAMIN

Even my full name is not my own. A Google search for "Benjamin David Philip Robinson," a name I use only on government identification, brings up one result:

Benjamin David Philip Robinson, our sweet baby boy, passed away Thursday, Oct. 14, 2010. He was the infant son of Shawn and Jenny Robinson of Sharon, Wis. He was brother to Dylan Tre, Ashton Kade, Shawn Thomas and Emalia Layla, all of Sharon, Wis. He is survived by his grandparents, Melanie Robinson, Edward and Betty (Gerambio) Kersting and Joseph Maxwell, all of Harvard; his great-grandmother, Barbara Gerambio of McHenry; his aunts and uncles, Eric and Lora Robinson of Wonder Lake, Philip Robinson Jr. of Delavan, Wis., Scott Robinson and Bridget Snell of Harvard; and his cousins, Trinida, Brook, Morgan, Riley, Evan, Luke and Conner. He was preceded in death by his grandpa, Philip "Papa Lucky" Robinson.

ROBINSON (CONTE ALMAVIVA), MEZZO-SOPRANO RAPHAELLA MEDINA (ROSINA), AND BASS-BARI-TONE TYLER BOUQUE (FIORELLO AND OFFICER). WE'VE SEEN HER LOCK LIPS WITH BEN ROBINSON, ADAM GLICK, AND CONRAD EMP-SON (AND MAYBE EVEN ROSS INIA?), AND WE LIKE HER STYLE! PRCA JACKSON, MISS. TIE-DOWN ROPING AVERAGE: 1. BLAKE ASH, 16.8 SECONDS ON TWO HEAD, $3,174; 2. TYLER MILLIGAN, 17.4, $2,760; 3. ZACK JONGBLOED, 17.5, $2,346; 4. TRENTON SMITH, 17.6, $1,932; 5. BO PICKETT, 17.8, $1,518; 6. HAVEN MEGED, 18.2, $1,104; 7. BEN ROBINSON, 18.5, $690; 8. BRAX-TON LAUGHLIN, 18.8, $276. NOV-ELTY PRIZE WINNERS INCLUDED BRETT MANNERS (LONG DRIVE ON THE 14TH), BRIAN RANDALL (LONG PUTT ON THE 15TH), MATTHEW WARBURTON, (BEST SECOND SHOT ON THE 13TH), AND BEN ROBINSON (NEAREST THE PIN ON THE 16TH). PINTEREST. BIKES. BENJAMIN ROB-INSON. WHAT MORE DO YOU NEED IN LIFE? BIKES, BEER, CUDDLE. BENJAMIN ROBINSON-DRAW-BRIDGE, RNZ PACIFIC JOURNAL-IST, TELLS US STAFF PROVIDING SERVICES TO REFUGEES ON

A friend who teaches kindergarten had two boys named Alex in her class. She said while the older Alex didn't show much interest in the younger Alex, the younger Alex thought their shared name bonded them.

To complicate matters further, the older Alex's best friend was named James which was the younger Alex's last name and so little Alex James followed Alex and James, determined they were meant to be friends.

To differentiate between them, the younger Alex had a "J" added to his name. He wrote Alex J on all his work. His parents wrote the J on the tags of his clothes. The J was written on his cubby. One morning, Alex J came into the classroom to find a name tag with only *Alex* written on it. "Where's my J?" he yelled. "Where's my J!"

MANUS ISLAND HAVE WALKED OFF THE JOB IN PROTEST. "CHRONIC HEALTH CONDITIONS REPRESENT 90% OF THE NATION'S 3.3 TRILLION ANNUAL HEALTH CARE EXPENDITURES," SAYS BEN ROBINSON, ZEEL'S SVP SALES. EARL BENJAMIN-ROBIN-SON, A HEALTH EQUITY STRATE-GIST FROM NEW ORLEANS, CLOSED OUT THE CONFERENCE WITH AN INSPIRATIONAL MES-SAGE REMINDING ATTENDEES ABOUT HOW IMPORTANT IT IS TO "WALK FEARLESSLY FOR-WARD TO FREEDOM AS BEST AS WE CAN." MINOR LEAGUE GOLF TOUR, THE EVERGREEN CLUB, PALM CITY: (FEB. 21) BEN ROBIN-SON, ENGLAND, $130.72 (37-35). IN OUR SECOND BLOG, DIREC-TOR OF AGENCY SERVICES, BEN ROBINSON, CONSIDERS HOW AGENTS COULD BE IDENTIFYING MONEY LAUNDERING RISK IN THEIR BUSINESS. THOSE LEFT TO CHERISH HIS MEMORIES ARE HIS CHILDREN, MICHAEL (ANGELA) WESTMORELAND AND SAMANTHA (BEN) ROBINSON OF JASPER, TN. BEN ROBINSON'S BACK-POST HEADER 12 MINUTES FROM TIME LOOKED LIKE IT HAD

At work, I overhear an adult ask a child what her new sibling's name is. The child freezes, just stands there until her mother jumps in to clarify that the newborn doesn't have a name yet, but they are considering a few. One is Nora.

Later that afternoon, another customer comes in and one of my coworkers asks what their last name is. The customer stares at my coworker for a moment before replying, "Don't have one" and walking away.

Later still, a customer comes in whose last name is Nobody.

RESCUED NEWMARKET A POINT, BUT THEY WERE PUNISHED FOR SOME SLACK DEFENDING IN THE FIRST MINUTE OF STOPPAGE TIME WHEN CAMERON RUSSELL TURNED THE BALL HOME. BEN ROBINSON, FROM TUNBRIDGE WELLS, SAYS HE WAS SUDDENLY MADE AWARE OF THE OBSTACLES DEAF PEOPLE FACE WHEN HE MET COLLEAGUE TOM FROUDE. "I DIDN'T EVEN REALIZE I HAD DONE ALL THAT UNTIL I SAW BEN'S STORY," WHITEMAN SAID, REFERRING TO BEN ROBINSON' STORY ABOUT HER ON GOBUCCS. COM. REVIEW OF *THE KID* (1921) BY BENJAMIN ROBINSON: MY FAVOURITE SCENES ARE GAR-BAGE FALLING ON CHARLIE, THE PANCAKE BREAKFAST THE PUGI-LISM, AND FINALLY THE ANGEL WINGS. IN OUR FINAL BLOG, DIRECTOR OF AGENCY SERVICES, BEN ROBINSON, CONSIDERS HOW TO PUT TOGETHER YOUR RISK ASSESSMENT AND WHAT STEPS YOU CAN PUT IN PLACE TO ENSURE YOU COMPLY WITH THE MONEY LAUNDERING REGULA-TIONS 2017. CHAIRMAN BEN ROB-INSON SAID: "AFTER WE MAN-AGED TO STAY IN THE

At work, I am required to wear a name tag with my first name on it. On the name tag, my name is shortened to Ben. The pages and shelfreaders' name tags display only their job title: Page/Shelfreader. The managers' name tags reveal their first and last names as well as their job title.

Sometimes patrons ask if my full first name is Benjamin. Then they ask if I know what my name means. These people are, almost always, Christians. They are surprised to find out I'm the oldest of two sons and not the youngest of twelve. They look at me as if I'm wearing the wrong name tag, wearing the name wrong.

CHAMPIONSHIP FOR A SECOND SEASON, WE KNEW WE WOULD HAVE TO INVEST AGAIN IN THE FIRST TEAM SQUAD TO GIVE US THE BEST CHANCE OF PUNCHING ABOVE OUR WEIGHT AND AVOIDING RELEGATION." REDCLIFFE DOLPHINS NAME TEAM FOR THE NORTHERN PRIDE INTRUST SUPER CUP CLASH INCLUDING DYLAN BRIGGS, GEOFFEREY PRINCE, DWIGHT SAUHEA, ISAIAH LEALIIEE, BEN ROBINSON-PATCH. IN 2011, 14-YEAR-OLD NORTHERN IRELAND SCHOOLBOY BEN ROBINSON DIED AFTER BEING ALLOWED TO PLAY ON DESPITE DEMONSTRATING CLEAR SIGNS HE'D SUFFERED A SIGNIFICANT BRAIN INJURY DURING AN ULSTER SCHOOLS GAME BETWEEN CARRICKFERGUS GRAMMAR AND DALRIADA. LAUGHTER FILLED THE SANCTUARY AS LONGTIME FRIENDS BOB VOEGELI, BOB DICKSON AND BEN ROBINSON SHARED MEMORIES OF GOLF GAMES AND IMPROMPTU TRIPS TO LAS VEGAS. UP THE OTHER END HOME GOALKEEPER MICHAEL BETT DID WELL TO KEEP OUT EFFORTS FROM BEN ROBINSON AND WHITEHEAD. EXPLORE BENJAMIN ROB-

Early on in his practice, a patient asked my dad, "What was your name before you changed it?" My dad was confused and asked the patient what he meant by the question. The patient asked what my dad's last name had been before he changed it to Robinson.

My dad's name is David. The patient thought our original last name was something like Rubinstein or Rubinsohn or Rabinowitz. Despite my dad's assurances that our family name had not been changed in recent memory, the patient asked what the names of his children were, as though to prove a point. I am Ben and my brother is Sam – Benjamin and Samuel.

Afterward, the patient's wife told my dad not to worry because she thought Jewish doctors were the smartest doctors anyway.

12 22'95

INSON'S 90 PHOTOS ON FLICKR! [LAUNCH OF NEW HERITAGE TRAIL IN FLINTSHIRE TOWN WITH THE HELP OF STUDENTS FROM ST RICHARD GWYN AND YSGOL CORNIST PARK ASSISTED IN DEVELOPING THE TRAIL BY TAKING PHOTOS, PRODUCING ARTWORK AND INTERVIEWING PEOPLE - PICTURED: CHAIR OF FCC PAUL CUNNINGHAM, CLLR CHRIS BITHEL, MP DAVID HANSON, FCC CHRIS REES JONES ALONG WITH ST RICHARD GWYN PUPILS JULIA HALAS, VILIUS FINKIS, ADAM GLOWACKI, BEN ROBINSON AND SANDRA DABROWSKI]. WHO IS BERNARD BENJAMIN ROBINSON? WAS BERNARD BENJAMIN ROBINSON ARRESTED? WHEN WAS BERNARD BENJAMIN ROBINSON ARRESTED? WHAT WAS BERNARD BENJAMIN ROBINSON ARRESTED FOR? IS THIS A MUGSHOT OF BERNARD BENJAMIN ROBINSON? ARE THERE MORE MUGSHOTS OF BERNARD BENJAMIN ROBINSON? IS THIS THE BERNARD BENJAMIN ROBINSON YOU KNOW? BERNARD BENJAMIN ROBINSON WAS BOOKED IN ORANGE COUNTY, FL. SO AFTER BERNARD BENJAMIN

Along with his ten half-brothers, Benjamin has one full brother, Joseph. Joseph is their father Jacob's favourite (a fact he flaunts) leading his half-brothers to become jealous and sell him into slavery in Egypt.

Unbeknownst to them, Joseph rises through the ranks, and when the brothers are forced to travel to Egypt for famine relief, they must deal with Joseph who they presumed was dead. Though they do not recognize him at first, he recognizes them immediately. He also realizes Benjamin has not made the trip with the others.

ROBINSON WAS DETAINED BY AUTHORITIES ON 03-09-2019, ALL OF THE INFORMATION FILED ON THAT DATE, AS WELL AS ALL FUTURE FILES DOCKETED IN CONNECTION WITH THE APPREHENSION OF BERNARD BENJAMIN ROBINSON IN ORANGE COUNTY, BECAME A MATTER OF PUBLIC RECORD. THAT IS WHY YOU ARE SEEING THIS REPORT ABOUT BERNARD BENJAMIN ROBINSON; THIS WEBSITE ENDEAVORS TO PUBLISH AN ACCURATE RECORD OF ALL DETAINMENTS IN ORANGE COUNTY TO BETTER PROVIDE FOR TRANSPARENCY IN GOVERNMENT. FOR AN UPDATE ON THE DETAINMENT OF BERNARD BENJAMIN ROBINSON, YOU ARE WELCOME TO CONTACT THE ORANGE COUNTY CLERK OF COURTS. THE INCLUSION OF INFORMATION REGARDING BERNARD BENJAMIN ROBINSON ON OUR WEBSITE IS AN INDICATION MERELY OF AN APPREHENSION. IN THE UNITED STATES, EVERYONE DETAINED BY A LAW ENFORCEMENT OFFICIAL, INCLUDING BERNARD BENJAMIN ROBINSON IS PRESUMED INNOCENT. BERNARD BENJAMIN ROBINSON'S NAME

One Saturday morning, when Sam was three years old, he wandered out of the house. My mom had gone for a walk and my dad was reading the paper and I was watching cartoons in the backroom and Sam simply walked out the front door.

I remember my dad coming to ask if I had seen Sam. I remember the panic creeping into my parents as it took longer and longer to find him. I remember us and our neighbours out searching, me still in my pyjamas.

AND/OR IMAGE APPEAR(S) HEREIN BECAUSE IT/THEY ARE PART OF THE ORANGE COUNTY CLERK OF COURT'S OFFICIAL RECORD AND ARE PUBLISHED IN ACCORDANCE WITH ALL LOCAL AND STATE LAWS IN THE STATE OF FLORIDA (USA). CONSOLIDATED CHARITY CHAIRMAN BEN ROBINSON SAID: "THIS IS OUR FIRST GRANTS MEETING OF THE YEAR AND WE RECEIVED A LARGE NUMBER OF APPLICATIONS FROM A VERY DIVERSE GROUP OF ORGANIZATIONS." BEN ROBINSON, LUCIA HERNANDEZ, AISLING FARRELL AND SEAN CULLIGAN WON A GRANT OF €1,000 FOR THEIR DESIGN OF A MICRO-BIT MOISTURE MONITOR WHICH INVOLVED CREATING AN AUTOMATIC PLANT WATERING SYSTEM. SHE IS SURVIVED BY HER HUSBAND: GERALD WILLIAM ROBINSON, WHOM SHE MARRIED JAN. 10, 1976; TWO DAUGHTERS: NANCY JANE ROBINSON OF LITCHFIELD, ILL., AND GINA (DAN) MCCULLEY OF BYRNES MILL; A BROTHER: ROBERT F. (MICHELLE ANN) SELF JR. OF DE SOTO; EIGHT GRANDCHILDREN: EMILEE G. (TROY) LONG,

When the brothers introduce themselves to Joseph, they explain they are "twelve brothers, the sons of one man, who lives in the land of Canaan. The youngest is now with our father, and one is no more."

Joseph responds by accusing them of being spies. He tells them in order to prove they are trustworthy, they must travel home, retrieve their brother Benjamin and return with him to Egypt. Otherwise, there will be no food for them.

GAVIN MIDDLETON, SAMUEL MIDDLETON, JOSEPH MIDDLE-TON, BENJAMIN ROBINSON, KIRSTEN (JAYMES BROOKSHIRE) CATES, HAYLEY CATES AND HANNAH MCCULLEY; AND NUMEROUS NIECES, NEPHEWS, COUSINS AND FRIENDS. BEN ROBINSON AND MICHELLE CHENEY FROM MICHAEL ROBINSON REAL ESTATE PRESENT A SPONSORSHIP CHEQUE TO MAGPIES PRESIDENT MATTHEW COLEMAN. RED CLIFFE DOLPHINS LINE-UP: 1. DYLAN BRIGGS 2. GEOFFREY PRINCE 3. DWIGHT SAUEHA 5. NATHAN DAWES 6. BEN ROBINSON-PATCH 7. HUDSON JONES 8. ZACHARY KERR 9. JAYDEN NEWBOULD 10. PATRICK RANDALL 11. JESSE JENNINGS 12. LACHLAN CHARD 13. OWEN JONES 14. MALYCHE TAFILI 16. HUNTER SMALLHORN 19. THOMPSON-REED KARENA 20. MANFRED BABAO 23. DANE PRATT. THE COMPANY'S CANADIAN PARENT HAS BEEN GRANTED PROTECTION FROM ITS CREDITORS WHILE IT RESTRUCTURES, WHICH THE GROUPS SAY WILL LEAD IT TO SELLING ITS PNG LICENSES ACCORDING TO BEN

Eventually, a family of four found Sam two blocks away and kept him with them until my dad made it that far.

When he saw Sam, my dad ran up and hugged him. Once they released, the mother stepped forward, looked my brother in the eye and asked, "Is this your dad?"

ROBINSON DRAWBRIDGE. LISTEN TO BENJAMIN ROBINSON - WHAT DO YOU SEEK? AND 65 OTHER EPISODES BY ARK MINISTRIES OF BERKELEY. AFTER A FAILED ATTEMPT TO SELL THE BUSINESS IN 2017, OWNER BEN ROBINSON HAS FINALLY SECURED A BUYER, AND WOUND DOWN HIS OWNERSHIP OF THE BUSINESS IN FEBRUARY. FROM THE FIELDS' BEN ROBINSON OUTLINES HOW ENERGY REVOLUTION IS HELPING THE LIVE EVENTS INDUSTRY TACKLE THE ENVIRONMENTAL IMPACTS OF TRAVEL. BEN ROBINSON, A TISBURY PLANNING BOARD MEMBER WHO HAS TRAVELED TO WASHINGTON WITH HIS FAMILY TO SUPPORT THE GREEN NEW DEAL AND WHOSE CHILDREN HAVE BEEN STRIKING FOR CLIMATE CHANGE AWARENESS, PRESSED KEATING, WHO HAS ENDORSED THE IDEA, TO DO MORE. REDCLIFFE DOLPHINS (20) TRIES: DWIGHT SAUEHA, ZACHARY KERR, AMANI ARUTAHIKI, BEN ROBINSON-PATCH. IT IS NOW EIGHT YEARS SINCE CARRICKFERGUS SCHOOLBOY BEN ROBINSON DIED FROM BRAIN INJURIES RECEIVED ON THE

The brothers return to Canaan and explain the situation to their father who immediately refuses to let Benjamin make the journey. Jacob is adamant that, after losing Rachel and Joseph, Benjamin's death would be the end of him.

Reuben goes so far as to promise Jacob the lives of his two sons if Benjamin does not return, but Jacob declines, saying, "My son will not go down there with you; his brother is dead and he is the only one left. If harm comes to him on the journey you are taking, you will bring my gray head down to the grave in sorrow."

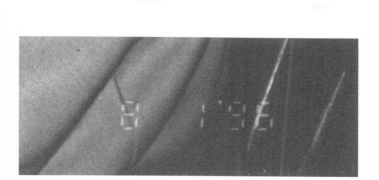

PITCH, BUT THE GOVERNING BODIES STILL HAVE NOT FOUND A WAY TO MAKE THE GAME SAFER FOR PLAYERS. SHINN SWITCHED THE BALL WIDE TO THE RIGHT FOR BEN ROBINSON, WHO WAITED FOR BLAKE KICKS TO GO BEYOND HIM ON THE OVERLAP. AFTER BEN ROBINSON EARNED THEM 1-1 DRAW AT CRICKET FIELD ROAD, NEWMARKET WENT OUT 4-2 ON PENALTIES, SHATTERING DREAMS OF A THIRD FINAL IN SIX YEARS. RUNNERS UP INCLUDE ANNA REM, RILEY OLSON, LAUREN WHYTE, PARKER HAWKINSON, BEN ROBINSON, AND JOSEPH ROBINSON. IN 2011, 14-YEAR-OLD BEN ROBINSON DIED AFTER SUSTAINING A HEAD INJURY DURING A RUGBY MATCH AND HIS FATHER EXPRESSED HIS DISMAY AT SATURDAY'S OFFICIATING ON TWITTER. ACTS 14 | FIX THE HOLE IN YOUR FAITH: A MESSAGE DELIVERED BY BENJAMIN ROBINSON AT OUR EMERYVILLE CAMPUS. AND ALBION CHAIRMAN BEN ROBINSON CONFIRMED THEY WOULD TAKE "A POSITIVE LOOK" AT THE POSSIBILITY AGAIN THIS TIME AROUND. BENJAMIN ROBINSON,

Growing up, I slept in a bunk bed. My brother and I had separate rooms, so sometimes I slept on the top bunk and sometimes on the bottom.

Often, on weekends, or in the summer, my brother slept in my room, but eventually I would be back in there alone, climbing up and down the ladder, an empty bed either above or below me.

GRINDING THE MOCKS: A THEORY OF MOCK DRAFTS, IN WHICH I DEVELOP A THEORY OF MOCK DRAFTS AND EXPLAIN WHY I AM INTERESTED IN USING THEM AS A WAY TO PREDICT THE NFL DRAFT. BEN ROBINSON SAYS BURTON ALBION'S TWO SEASONS IN THE CHAMPIONSHIP HAVE GIVEN THE CLUB "MORE REALISTIC EXPECTATIONS OF THE LEVEL OF SUPPORT WE CAN GET." DALLAS MORNING NEWS OUTTAKES: BENJAMIN ROBINSON COVERS DEEP ELLUM PROTEST. ROBINSON PROPERTY'S BEN ROBINSON IS MARKETING A SIZEABLE PENTHOUSE IN THE ROYAL COMPLEX WITH A PRICE GUIDE OF $3.85 MILLION. "THE GLOBAL DIGITAL BANKING MARKET IS EXPECTED TO REACH NEARLY $9 TRILLION (USD) BY 2025, AND THIS EXPANSION IS DRIVEN BY THE OPPORTUNITY TO PROVIDE NEW SERVICES IN NEW MARKETS," SAID BEN ROBINSON, TEMENOS CHIEF STRATEGY OFFICER & HEAD OF MARKETPLACE. HE HAS ESPECIALLY THANKED BUSINESSMEN BEN ROBINSON AND MALCOLM PRENTICE FOR THEIR CONTINUOUS SUPPORT HELPING HIM

Only after the famine persists and the family is at risk of starving, does Jacob relent and agree to let Benjamin make the journey to Egypt with his brothers.

When the brothers arrive with Benjamin in tow, Joseph replenishes their food stores as promised. However, as they are preparing to return home, Joseph puts his next plot into action.

Joseph tells his servant to hide a silver cup in Benjamin's bag as the brothers are preparing to leave. Once they depart, Joseph sends his servants after the brothers to tell them whoever is found with the silver cup must become his slave.

When it is revealed that the cup is in Benjamin's bag, the brothers all tear their clothes and beg Joseph to take any of them in Benjamin's place.

RAISE MONEY FOR VARIOUS GOOD CAUSES. SHELTON INTERMEDIATE SCHOOL HAS ANNOUNCED THE FIRST QUARTER HIGH HONORS AND HONOR ROLLS. CONGRATULATIONS TO ALS GRADUATION CLASS 19-C, 75TH COMMUNICATIONS & INFORMATION DIRECTORATE: BENJAMIN ROBINSON. AND BEN ROBINSON, THE CLUB CHAIRMAN, SAYS THE JOURNEY WILL BE ETCHED INTO THE CLUB'S HISTORY. "A CLOUD-FIRST SECURITY STRATEGY IS NOT ONLY DESIRABLE FOR SPEED-TO-MARKET AND FLEXIBILITY, BUT IS ALSO A REQUIREMENT FOR COMPLIANCE IN MANY CASES," SAID BEN ROBINSON, THE CHIEF STRATEGY OFFICER & HEAD OF THE TEMENOS MARKETPLACE. SAM GOMARSALL LED THE WAY FOR THE JOCKEYS WITH A HAT-TRICK, WHILE BEN ROBINSON NETTED TWICE AND JACK WHITING - WITH A 30 YARD STUNNER - AND LEWIS WHITEFILED WERE ALSO ON THE SCORESHEET. ACTS 15 | THE WITNESS OF THE SPIRIT, SPEAKER: BENJAMIN ROBINSON, SAN FRANCISCO CAMPUS, 7/4/2019, FREE, VIEW IN ITUNES. SAMUEL ALSO

The first time I remember seeing my dad cry was at the back of the church.

For some reason, I had been flipping through the guest book. Not that I would have known the date, but I flipped in the book to the day of Emily's memorial service.

I left the book open to that page before running off with my brother. When my dad came in to collect us, the book caught his eye and he got very quiet.

QUIZZED BURTON ALBION FC
CHIEF, BEN ROBINSON, WHO IS
ONE OF JUST A HANDFUL OF
BLACK, ASIAN, AND MINORITY
ETHNIC (BAME) CHAIRMEN IN
THE ENGLISH FOOTBALL LEAGUE.
ANDREW OSTLE HELPED HIM-
SELF TO A HAT-TRICK AND WAS
NAMED ELLENBOROUGH'S MAN
OF THE MATCH AND HE WAS FOL-
LOWED OVER THE SEATON LINE
BY BEN ROBINSON, LUKE PEN-
RICE, MATTHEW BELL, ZAC
OLSTRUM AND KAI GILHESPY.
THERE IS ALSO STILL JUST THE
ONE BRITISH CHAIRMAN OF A
CLUB, BEN ROBINSON AT LEAGUE
ONE BURTON ALBION, WHO IS
FROM AN AFRICAN AND CARIB-
BEAN BACKGROUND. GALLERY 4
ART EXHIBITION - BEN ROBINSON
- POETRY – $5/FT. CENTRAL - 1ST
FLOOR GALLERY 4. BEN ROBIN-
SON, 24, SUFFERED WITH
ANOREXIA NERVOSA FROM THE
AGE OF 15, AND AS A RESULT,
SPENT A YEAR AS AN INPATIENT
IN A SPECIALISED ADOLESCENT
UNIT. BEN ROBINSON, A MEMBER
OF THE TISBURY PLANNING
BOARD, SAID THE BOARD OF
SELECTMEN TAKING NO ACTION
ON THE FUNDS WOULD ESSEN-

When Judah's plea does not convince Joseph, Benjamin makes a plea of his own swearing, "As truly as my brother Joseph is separated from me, as truly as he has been made a slave, I have not touched the cup."

Joseph asks Benjamin to prove that his brother's memory is significant enough for Joseph to take Benjamin at his word. At this point, Benjamin reveals he has recorded his brother's story in the same way his mother and father recorded theirs – by documenting it in the names of the next generation.

TIALLY BE AN ENDORSEMENT OF THE ENTIRE TRACK AND FIELD PROJECT. JOE ROSE BAGGED TWO FOR THE VICTORS, WHOSE OTHER GOALS CAME COURTESY OF AL WRAY, BEN ROBINSON AND MAN OF THE MATCH MAX LOY. BEN ROBINSON ALSO BAGGED A BRACE FOR THE JOCKEYS, WHILE LEWIS WHITEHEAD AND JOE WHITING NETTED TOO. BREWERS CHAIRMAN BEN ROBINSON SAID: "WE ARE ALWAYS DELIGHTED TO WELCOME BURTON ROTARY CLUB TO THE PIRELLI STADIUM FOR THIS POPULAR EVENT." HIS BLOS-SOMING PARTNERSHIP WITH BEN ROBINSON CAME TO FRUITION ONCE AGAIN AS THE WINGER CUSHIONED A HEADER PER-FECTLY INTO WHITEHEAD'S PATH AND NEWMARKET'S NUMBER NINE DID THE REST WITH A COM-POSED FINISH FROM 12 YARDS OUT. "AS REPORTED ON SKY SPORTS NEWS YESTERDAY WE HAVE HAD OFFERS FROM FIVE FOOTBALL CLUBS TO SHARE WITH THEM, AND AS BURTON HAVE COME OUT AND CONFIRMED THEY ARE ONE OF THE CLUBS, I AM HAPPY TO SAY I DID RECEIVE CALL FROM CHAIRMAN BEN ROB-

Bela (swallow) because Joseph disappeared or was swallowed up.

Becher (firstborn) because Joseph was Rachel's first child.

Ashbel (capture) because God sent Joseph into captivity.

Gera (sojourner) because Joseph was in Egypt.

Naaman (pleasing) because of Joseph's eloquence.

Ehi (brother) because Joseph was Benjamin's only full brother.

Rosh (leader) because Joseph was Benjamin's elder.

Muppim (from the mouth) because Joseph passed on Jacob's teachings.

Huppim (marriage canopies) because Benjamin missed Joseph's wedding.

Ard (descend) because Joseph goes down to Egypt.

At the end of writing this, I read that the origin of Ben-Oni is closer to *son of my vigour* than *son of my sorrow.*

Is it like Mary Kim Arnold writes, "Maybe I misremember.

Maybe I want there to be more of a story than there is."

INSON, WHO I HAVE KNOWN FOR MANY YEARS, THEY HAVE KINDLY OFFERED US THEIR FACILITIES." GIVEN AN EXCELLENT RIDE BY APPRENTICE BEN ROBINSON, THE NINE-YEAR-OLD STAYED ON STRONGLY TO DENY SEMPRE PRESTO HER THIRD COURSE WIN. A HIGH BALL INTO THE BOX SAW BEN ROBINSON SHOVE BARNES OUT OF THE WAY TO HEAD GOAL-WARDS. PROFESSIONAL SOLOISTS FOR THE PROGRAM ARE MARIA FERRANTE, SOPRANO; PAMELA STEVENS, MEZZO-SOPRANO; BEN-JAMIN ROBINSON, TENOR, AND BRIAN MING-CHU, BARITONE. REQUITED JOURNAL ARCHIVE: PERFORMANCE, BENJAMIN ROB-INSON. BEN ROBINSON: JEREMY MCGOVERN, ESPECIALLY IF FREO DELIVER THE BALL INTO THE FOR-WARD LINE IN THEIR NOW-CUS-TOMARY FASHION. THERE WERE SEVEN REGISTERED BIDDERS FOR WHAT ROBINSON PROPERTY'S BEN ROBINSON DESCRIBED AS "A GREAT AUCTION" WHICH RESULTED IN A NEW PRICE HIGH FOR MEREWETHER'S FELLOWES STREET, ACCORDING TO AUSTRA-LIAN PROPERTY MONITORS DATA. AND DESPITE BURTON ALBION

Though Benjamin's great-grandfather Abram would eventually become the patriarch of the faith, much of his life was consumed with anxiety over his lack of an heir.

Late into their lives, Abram and his wife Sarai still do not have any children of their own. Despite divine assurance they will not remain childless, the couple is so consumed with their desire for offspring that they _____ Sarai's slave Hagar into carrying Abram's child.

What verb might describe what Abram and Sarai do to Hagar? When Hagar becomes pregnant with Abram's child, Sarai is enraged, despite it being her idea, and drives Hagar away.

CHAIRMAN BEN ROBINSON PRE-
VIOUSLY REVEALING THAT THEY
WOULD TAKE "A POSITIVE LOOK"
AT COVENTRY CITY'S PROPOSAL,
THEY ARE NO LONGER BELIEVED
TO BE ONE OF THE CLUBS
REFERRED TO IN YESTERDAY'S
STATEMENT RELEASED BY COV-
ENTRY CITY. STOWMARKET FELL
BEHIND IN THE 10TH MINUTE
AT NEWMARKET WHEN LEWIS
WHITEHEAD SMARTLY SIDE-
FOOTED IN BEN ROBINSON'S
KNOCKDOWN FROM 12 YARDS
OUT. IN ADDITION TO A GREAT
MEAL, YOU'LL BE TREATED TO
ITALIAN SOLO PERFORMANCES
BY SHS STATE SOLOISTS INCLUD-
ING SOPRANO HOPE AMBRIDGE,
MEZZO SOPRANO ANNA HUGHES
(FRENCH), MEZZO SOPRANO
KATHI KESSLER (GERMAN), ALTO
JAIDA DONALDSON, ALTO
MIKAYLA SCHOENING (ENGLISH),
TENOR BURTON ANDERSON,
TENOR RILEY ANDERSON, BARI-
TONE IGNACIO PADILLA, BARI-
TONE JOEL JOHNSON, BASS BEN
ROBINSON, BARITONE ZANE
RASOR (PORTUGESE), AND BASS
FREDDY LIBBY. HE GOT INTO THE
BACK OF A CAR WHICH WAS
DRIVEN BY FINCH AND IN WHICH

Each year, on April 30th, my parents would take my brother and me to the children's memorial garden at the church. We would weed and plant and collect trash that had blown in from the road.

During these visits, my brother and I would help with the work for a while before running off to play elsewhere on the property – climbing the pine trees or wrestling on the lawn.

On the opposite side of the church, there were deep window wells cut into the parking lot to let light into the basement of the church hall. The window wells were enclosed by metal railings with chipped black paint. My brother and I would hang from the railings and then drop down below the surface of the parking lot, wait in the wells for our parents to retrieve us.

SIDEKICKS OLIVER DWYER AND BEN ROBINSON WERE PASSENGERS. BENJAMIN ROBINSON - APPLE - WORSHIP SET LIST: FOREVERNO OTHER SAVIOR MERCY LIVING HOPE. KAYLEE HUGHES (RUTH), BENJAMIN ROBINSON (FREDRICK) AND JACK SEAGUE (PIRATE KING) SING TO THE BALCONY IN THE SECOND ACT OF PIRATE'S OF PENZANCE. THE VOCAL STRENGTH OF THE ENTIRE CAST IS REMARKABLE, WITH STAND-OUT PERFORMANCES BY KAYLEE HUGHES AS RUTH, TYLER MCKENZIE AS THE MAJOR GENERAL, JACK SEAGUE AS THE PIRATE KING, MEGAN VAUGHN AS MABEL AND GUEST ARTIST BENJAMIN ROBINSON SINGING TENOR AS FREDERICK, OUR STORY'S HERO. STUDENTS WERE GIVEN A CHANCE TO WORK WITH A VISITING TENOR, BENJAMIN ROBINSON, WHO HAS PERFORMED FREDERICK IN OVER FORTY VENUES AND GAVE THE FINAL PROFESSIONAL FLOURISHES TO THIS 2018-19 CAPSTONE TO REMEMBER. STITT ANNOUNCED ON MONDAY HIS SELECTION OF RETIRED AIR FORCE BRIG. GEN. BEN ROBINSON TO THE CABINET POST

The tree Emily's ashes were buried under was a pussywillow – the common name for three different types of willows native to Europe, Asia and North America. The tree has the traditional weeping connotation of the willow but there is a unique softness to the plant's fuzzy buds.

The bark and leaves of willows contain a chemical known as salicin, a natural painkiller and the historical source of aspirin.

On a Sunday afternoon a couple of years ago, my parents went to work in the garden at the church and found the pussywillow had been cut down level with the dirt. When they asked the groundskeeper about it, he said the tree was dead and needed to be removed.

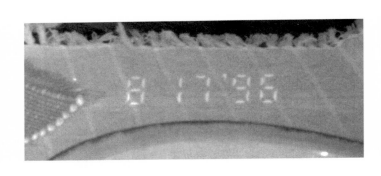

9 11'96

THAT REQUIRES SENATE CON-
FIRMATION. THE PHOTO ALSO
INCLUDED CHEF BEN ROBINSON,
LEADING MANY TO SPECULATE
THAT HE MIGHT BE JOINING THE
CREW THIS SEASON. ELLENBOR-
OUGH WON WELL WITH TRIES
FROM MAN OF THE MATCH BEN
ROBINSON (2), KEVIN HOBAN,
OWEN HOYLES, NIALL GRAY, KAI
GILHESPY AND RHYS BURR.
MORE THAN A MOMENT –
SPEAKER: BENJAMIN ROBIN-
SON, EMERYVILLE CAMPUS.
FINCH, 36, OF CARRANT ROAD,
TEWKESBURY, DWYER, 30, OF
BANTOCK ROAD, HARBORNE,
BIRMINGHAM, AND BEN ROBIN-
SON, 22, OF NORTH BOUNDARY
ROAD, BRIXHAM, ALL ADMIT-
TED SUPPLY AND POSSESSION OF
HEROIN AND COCAINE WITH
INTENT TO SUPPLY. OFF-SPINNER
BEN ROBINSON HAS RETURNED
TO THE CLUB WHERE HE
STARTED HIS CAREER ALONG
WITH FELLOW TWEAKER DAN
VERNON. HOWEVER, THE WALL
IS DESCRIBED BY DR BEN ROBIN-
SON, TV PRESENTER AND A PRIN-
CIPAL ADVISER TO HERITAGE
ENGLAND, AS ONE OF THE TOP 25
MOST IMPORTANT SCHEDULED

When Abram is ninety-nine years old, and his and Hagar's son Ishmael is twelve years old, God again appears to Abram and says, "No longer will you be called Abram; your name will be Abraham, for I have made you a father of many nations."

God also tells Abram that Sarai's name will now be Sarah.

One year later, Sarah gives birth to a son – Isaac.

MONUMENTS IN THE COUNTRY, OTHERS ON THE LIST INCLUDE STONEHENGE. AN OUTBREAK OF TYPHOID FEVER HAS STRUCK REFUGEES DETAINED BY AUSTRALIA ON PAPUA NEW GUINEA'S MANUS ISLAND REPORTS BENJAMIN ROBINSON-DRAWBRIDGE. HE IS PARTNERED BY BEN ROBINSON WHO TAKES OFF A VALUABLE 3LB. SENIOR BEN ROBINSON IS THE SON OF JASON AND KATHY ROBINSON OF WINONA. DETECTIVE SERGEANT BEN ROBINSON, FROM HUMBERSIDE POLICE'S ECONOMIC CRIME UNIT, HAS PLEDGED TO TACKLE THE RISE IN THE NUMBER OF ROMANCE FRAUD OFFENCES AND SAYS PREVENTION IS THE KEY. "THE TEAM BETWEEN MOQDIGITAL, LAING O'ROURKE AND NUTANIX WORKED REALLY WELL TOGETHER TO SECURE AND ENSURE THE SUCCESS OF THIS DEPLOYMENT," MOQDIGITAL SALES MANAGER BEN ROBINSON TOLD CRN. HAPPY TO SIDE WITH THE BEN ROBINSON TRAINED 9 ALFIE JUNIOR. I'M KEEN TO SEE THE BEN ROBINSON TRAINED 12 SPORTINI GOING CLOSE TO WINNING. PICTURED IN THE TOP ROW ARE BURTON

My wife, my son and I go to the church on what would have been Emily's 25th birthday. The property is bleak. It is a grey, windy day. The church has installed security cameras on many of the outer walls. The window wells are now covered with tinted plastic.

The garden is sparse even for early spring – the mulch gone patchy, the grass encroaching. The masonry on the abutting cinder block wall is beginning to fail, bowing beneath the safety grate.

The stump of the pussywillow tree is still there, still lodged in the soil when I pull on it. I remove a piece of bark and slip it into my pocket.

ANDERSON, IGNACIO PADILLA, AND BEN ROBINSON. HOST ANDY COHEN ASKED ROSBACH TO CHOOSE BETWEEN CHEF BEN ROBINSON OR MARTIN'S COOKING. "GEN. BEN ROBINSON BRAVELY SERVED OUR COUNTRY IN THE UNITED STATES AIR FORCE, AND CONTINUES TO CONTRIBUTE TO OKLAHOMA'S VETERANS AND MILITARY COMMUNITY EVERY DAY," SAID STITT. BEN ROBINSON, DIRECTOR OF AGENCY SERVICES, LANDMARK INFORMATION, SAYS, "THERE ARE PLENTY OF CASE STUDIES TO BACK UP THE SUCCESS OF LOCAL AGENT GROWTH THROUGH LOCAL PROPERTY MARKET DATA." THAT BOOSTS A SIDE WHICH HAS LOST THE LIKES OF CHARLIE STAINES (PENRITH), BEN ROBINSON (RETIRED), FARREN LAMB (OBERON TIGERS), JARRED TYACK (ORANGE CYMS), AND TRAIE MERRITT (BATHURST ST PAT'S). USING DATA FROM BENJA-MIN ROBINSON, WHO HAS CURATED CLOSE TO 2,000 MOCK DRAFTS FROM EXPERT, MEDIA AND FAN SOURCES FROM APRIL 2018 TO PRESENT, HERE ARE SOME OF THE MOST INTERESTING FLUC-TUATIONS OVER THE PAST FEW

After waiting her whole life for a child, Sarah gives birth to Isaac. At some point after the birth – it is unclear how long – God commands her husband to take Isaac away and sacrifice him.

Together, with two of Abraham's young men, he and Isaac make the three-day journey to the land of Moriah. When they see the place where Isaac is to be sacrificed, Abraham leaves his two men and heads off with his son, the wood, the knife and the fire.

As they approach the mountain, Isaac turns to Abraham and asks where the lamb is for their sacrifice. Abraham's reply is cryptic: "God himself will provide the lamb for the burnt offering, my son."

MONTHS — ALONG WITH SOME OF OUR OWN ANALYSIS MIXED IN. BEN ROBINSON OF LEHMAN, PA. WAS SECOND IN THIS YEAR'S 25K, AT TWO HOURS, 15 MINUTES, WHILE TYLER STINSON OF TUCSON, ARIZONA, CAME IN THIRD WITH A TIME OF TWO HOURS, 33 MINUTES. "THIS ENDS UP WITH A LOT OF FRAGMENTATION BETWEEN THE OPEN SPACE," SAID COMMISSIONER BEN ROBINSON. "WHEREAS YOU COULD ACCOMPLISH REAL OPEN SPACE WITH A LARGE, SEGREGATED LOT THAT IS PROTECTED." I GOT INTO TORQUAY LATE MORNING WITH A PAL, WALKED TO THE SEA FRONT AND FOUND BEN ROBINSON LOOKING OUT TO SEA. BENJAMIN ROBINSON, A FORMER MISSISSIPPI DEPT. OF HEALTH WORKER WHO HELPED BATON ROUGE'S METRO HEALTH GET ITS RED WIG WALK STARTED, SPEAKS DURING THE SIXTH ANNUAL RED WIG WALK, HELD TO RAISE AWARENESS OF HIV PREVENTION, TREATMENT AND SUPPORT SERVICES, SATURDAY, APRIL 27, 2019. "THIS IS A DYNAMIC COMBINATION OF AN EXPERT CREATIVE STAFF WORK-

The only sign of Emily in the church garden is a stone, a piece of granite about the size of a soccer ball, with a plaque attached to it that reads:

CHILDREN'S MEMORIAL GARDEN
1996

In the centre, an excerpt from Elizabeth Barrett Browning's "Sonnet 43" – two lines that, here, are drawn out into three:

I love thee with the
breath, smiles, tears,
of all my life.

Later, I find the rest of the poem and see, where the plaque has a period, the original has a semi-colon; out beyond that full stop, the poem concludes, "and, if God choose, /I shall but love thee better after death."

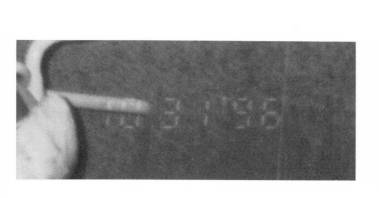

ING CLOSELY WITH AN ENGAGED CLIENT," STATES BEN ROBINSON, PRESIDENT. ARCHIVE HAS WON TWICE FOR JOCKEY BEN ROBINSON, WHO IS AGAIN IN THE PLATE AFTER WINS AT PONTEFRACT AND BEVERLEY. IT WAS WRITTEN ON MCCLELLAN'S OFFICIAL STATIONERY, WHICH INCLUDED HIS IMAGE AND THAT OF PRESIDENT LINCOLN AND SEVERAL OTHER GENERALS, TO BENJAMIN ROBINSON OF GREENFIELD. AS SHE GAVE EVIDENCE IN THE CROWN'S CASE AGAINST DALTON BENJAMIN ROBINSON JR (21), THE WOMAN SAID THAT THE MAN WAS TRYING TO "SCARE AND INTIMIDATE" HER AS HE HAD A HAND ON WHAT SHE BELIEVED WAS THE WEAPON UNDER HIS SHIRT. FELLOW OPENER BEN ROBINSON WAS NOT OUT ON 56 AND MATTHEW BELL ON 35 WHEN THE CLIFTON PARKERS CROSSED THE WINNING LINE AFTER JUST 35.1 OVERS. BEN ROBINSON, PRESIDENT AND CEO OF ROSE HILL CENTER OF HOLLY, WAS NAMED ADMINISTRATOR OF THE YEAR BY THE NATIONAL ALLIANCE ON MENTAL ILLNESS (NAMI) MICHIGAN. TREVOR

When they reach the place for the sacrifice, Abraham prepares an altar, binding Isaac and laying him on top of the wood. Just as Abraham lifts the knife, an angel appears and tells him not to kill Isaac, that he has proven his faith.

Abraham finds a ram caught in some nearby bushes and sacrifices it before the passage ends abruptly stating, "Then Abraham returned to his servants, and they set off together for Beersheba. And Abraham stayed in Beersheba."

No mention of Isaac coming down the mountain. What did they tell the men? Did Isaac ever tell his own son about this day?

WALKER, KATE CHASTAIN, SIERRA STORM, BEN ROBINSON, CAPTAIN LEE ROSBACH, NICO SHOLLY, KELLEY JOHNSON, LAUREN BURCHELL, EMILY WARBURTON-ADAMS ARE SEEN IN A SEASON 4 PROMO SHOT. PARANOIA ABOUT ABDUCTIONS HAS GRIPPED THE CAPITAL, WHICH A SOCIAL COMMENTATOR SAYS MAY BE PART OF AN EFFORT TO FOMENT UNREST – BENJAMIN ROBINSON-DRAWBRIDGE HAS MORE. IN MEMORY OF BENJAMIN "BEN" PAUL ROBINSON. FORBES MAGPIES: 1 BAILEY HARTWIG, 2 KRISTIAN MARKWORT, 3 BRYDON RAMIEN, 4 ETHAN GAFFNEY, 5 WARREN BAXTER, 6 MITCH BURKE, 7 JORDAN HARTWIG, 8 BEN MAGUIRE, 9 JAIDEN BURKE, 10 BEN ROBINSON, 11 HAYDEN ROBINSON, 12 JAKE STENHOUSE, 13 HAYDEN BOLAM (C), 14 STUART KENNEDY, 15 MATTHEW ROYLANCE. BEN ROBINSON, CHIEF STRATEGY OFFICER OF TEMENOS, HAS LEFT THE COMPANY. THE ADVOCATE IAN RINTOUL TOLD BEN ROBINSON DRAWBRIDGE THE CONDITION OF THE REFUGEES HAS WORSENED SINCE HE WAS LAST ON THE ISLAND SIX

My parents tell me that the year after Emily's death, I asked to have a birthday party for her. Not wanting to impede whatever strange path grief might be taking, they agreed.

My grandmother and I baked the cake together – mixed the batter, poured it into a tray, watched it rise, frosted the top.

This is one of the days no photographs were taken. Was anything written on the cake? Did someone blow out candles? Did we sing?

MONTHS AGO. DAVID MANARA (LAWRENCE) HAD 27 REPS ON THE BENCH PRESS, WITH BENJAMIN ROBINSON (YORKTOWN) POSTING 24 REPS. BELOW DECK'S CHEF BEN ROBINSON HAS AN UPDATE ON HIS LOCATION THESE DAYS: "REALLY BUSY!" AFTER HE GAVE UP YACHT LIFE BACK IN 2017, BELOW DECK ALUM BEN ROBINSON HAS BROUGHT HIS CULINARY PROWESS TO KITCHENS THAT, WELL, DON'T FLOAT. EXEC PRODUCER - BEN ROBINSON, PROUD ROBINSON & PARTNERS. WORKING WITH BEST-OF-BREED PARTNERS, SUCH AS THE VALPAL NETWORK, COMPLEMENTS BOTH PRODUCT PORTFOLIOS AND ENABLES US TO SUPPORT OUR CLIENTS' SALES PIPELINES AS WELL AS ADDRESSING THEIR COMPLIANCE, DUE DILIGENCE AND PROPERTY LISTING NEEDS" EXPLAINS BEN ROBINSON, MANAGING DIRECTOR OF LANDMARK ESTATE AGENCY SERVICES. IRVINE (18) AND SKIPPER RYAN LEWIS (27) PUT A TEMPORARY HALT TO THE COLLAPSE WITH A RUN-A-BALL STAND OF 26, AND LEWIS AND BEN ROBINSON THEN SCROUNGED ANOTHER 23

Not long before Benjamin is born, a figure comes to Jacob in the night and begins to wrestle with him. Robert Alter calls the figure "the man who was no man." The two are evenly matched and they struggle all through the night until the sun comes up.

As day breaks, the figure tells Jacob to let him go but Jacob insists the figure bless him first. The figure then asks Jacob what his name is, before immediately responding, "Your name will no longer be Jacob, but Israel, because you have struggled with God and with humans and have overcome."

As the figure goes to leave, Jacob asks, "Please tell me your name," to which the figure replies, "Why do you ask my name?"

FOR THE NINTH WICKET, BUT NOTTS 224 PROVED A TARGET TOO FAR. 6 MAY 2019: DIVINE GUIDANCE - SPEAKER: BENJAMIN ROBINSON, EMERYVILLE CAMPUS. BEN ROBINSON TALKS ABOUT "ADAPTATION" EFFORTS FROM HIS WORKING GROUP DISCUSSION. "THE MORE WE CAN PROVIDE FOR OURSELVES ON THE ISLAND, THE LESS WE NEED TO BRING IN FROM THE MAINLAND," SAID BEN ROBINSON, WHO PRESENTED ON BEHALF OF THE ADAPTATION WORKING GROUP. DURING THE PAST 17 YEARS, WE'VE HAD THE PLEASURE OF WORKING WITH TOP CELEBRITY CHEFS LIKE GUY FIERI, MICHAEL SYMON, TONY LUKE, AND BEN ROBINSON. HERE ARE THE RESULTS, PERSONAL FINISHER CERTIFICATE AND FINISH LINE VIDEO FOR BENJAMIN ROBINSON WHO COMPLETED THE HULL MARATHON 2017 RESULTS. LOOKING GOOD BENJAMIN ROBINSON. MAGPIES: 1 BAILEY HARTWIG, 2 KRISTIAN MARKWORT, 3 HAYDEN ROBINSON, 4 ETHAN GAFFNEY, 5 WARREN BAXTER, 6 MITCHELL BURKE, 7 JORDAN HARTWIG, 8 BEN MAGUIRE, 9 HAYDEN BOLAM,

When my parents were expecting me, they had two names picked out: Benjamin and Annie.

Did my parents think of Annie in the months before I was born? In the months after? Picture themselves holding a baby girl? Later on, when my parents were expecting my sister, they did not come back to Annie.

10 BEN ROBINSON, 11 TIMOTHY DUKES, 12 JAKE STENHOUSE, 13 JAKE HADDRILL, 14 JAIDEN BURKE, 15 JACK HARTWIG, 16 MATTHEW ROYLANCE, 17 JOSH TOOLE. COACH: CAMERON GREEN-HALGH. FRONTED BY AWARD-WINNING UK MUSIC FESTIVAL FOUNDER OF BLUEDOT AND KENDAL CALLING BEN ROBINSON, THIS COLLECTIVE BEGAN AS AN EXPERIMENTAL STUDIO PROJECT WITH OVER 50 COLLABORATORS. THE IDEA FOR THE RE-ENVISIONED FRAMEWORK CAME FROM RAYLYNMOR OPERA ARTISTIC DIRECTOR, BENJAMIN ROBINSON, WHO WROTE THE NEW ENGLISH LIBRETTO. EXCERPT FROM LAY-CRAFT EXEMPLIFIED IN A DISCOVERY OF THE WEAKNESS OF THE LATE ATTEMPTS OF THE AUTHOR OF PRIEST-CRAFT IN PERFECTION AND MR. BENJAMIN ROBINSON, MINISTER OF THE GOSPEL, TO PROVE THE ENGLISH CLERGY GUILTY OF FORGERY: IN A LETTER TO MR. ROBINSON. MEMORIZE, MEDITATE, AND PRAY YOUR THROUGH THE BIBLE WITH PASTOR BENJAMIN ROBINSON. ROBINSON PROPERTY'S BEN ROBIN-

Shortly after my son was born, the midwife placed a bracelet around his wrist with GELEYNSE, BABY MALE ALLISON printed on it.

Before his birth, Allison and I had already decided on his name, but until then, the name had only been a thought, an idea. We had discussed it, spoken it aloud, but it wasn't documented anywhere.

The morning after he was born, I went down to the hospital clerk's office and they had me fill out several forms.

The last form I filled out was for his temporary health card – a simple slip of paper with a dotted line inside a box where I was to write his name. As I held the blue ballpoint pen above the line, I felt myself hesitate for just a second.

SON IS SELLING A ONE-BEDROOM UNIT AT 7/21 RANCLAUD STREET WITH A GUIDE OF $390,000 TO $410,000. THE BATTLE-HARDENED NINE-YEAR-OLD WAS GIVEN PLENTY TO DO TOWARDS THE TAIL OF THE FIELD BY YOUNG BEN ROBINSON. BEN ROBINSON, TAP CENTRE FOR CREATIVITY, 203 DUNDAS STREET, LONDON, ONTARIO N6A 1G4, LONDON, CANADA. TIE-DOWN ROPING LEADERS: 1. (TIE) BEN ROBINSON AND SHANE SMITH 8.5 SECONDS EACH; 3. (TIE) SHANE HANCHEY AND RILEY WARREN, 9.3 EACH; 5. DARREN DUBLANKO, 10.9; 6. MORGAN GRANT, 11.3; 7. CURTIS CASSIDY, 11.5; 8. AARON MOSICKI, 12.1. UNIMAGINEABLE, TRAINED BY BEN ROBINSON, WAS BEATEN 6.1L INTO EIGHTH PLACE, CARRYING THE NO.4 SADDLECLOTH. GARY MAYOR KAREN FREEMAN-WILSON, RIGHT, GETS SOME EARLY NUMBERS FROM 4TH DISTRICT PRECINCT CAPTAIN BEN ROBINSON AT HER ELECTION PARTY IN THE POPOVICH HANGAR AT THE GARY/CHICAGO INTERNATIONAL AIRPORT. OVER IN THE WORLD OF PROPERTY INDUSTRY SUPPLIERS, LANDMARK INFORMATION GROUP HAS ANNOUNCED THAT BEN ROBINSON HAS BEEN

A week later, I apply for his permanent health card and birth certificate. I fill out a form that includes the following:

The parents agree to this legal name: [ ]

Number of live born children to this [ ]
  parent, including this birth: (A)

Number of stillborn (not born alive) [ ]
  children born to this parent: (B)

Total number of children [ ]
  born to this parent: (A+B)

When the documents arrive in the mail, they come addressed to my son.

ACKNOWLEDGEMENTS

Jim Johnstone for seeing the book.

Aimée Parent Dunn for making it happen.

Gary Barwin for some key conversations.

Steacy for reading every version.

Aaron Schneider and Amy Mitchell of The Temz Review for publishing an excerpt.

Kyle Flemmer and rob mclennan of *GUEST* for publishing a different excerpt.

Noelle Allen at Wolsak & Wynn for funding the writing through the Ontario Arts Council.

Joe, Josh and John for notes.

Mark and Kira for introducing me to Alter.

Rob and Nate for help with the Hebrew.

Rob and Jamie for space to write and read and live.

Karley for a story.

Ben M for wearing the name with me.

Jenna, Shanika and Erica for bringing us Jim;

Elise and Olivia for bringing us Lou.

My parents for being willing.

My grandparents for the stories.

Allison, Jim and Lou for living it with me.

NOTES

The epigraph is from bpnichol's "Two Words: A Wedding."

The Robert Alter quotations are from *The Five Books of Moses*.

All biblical quotations are from the New International Version.

Benjamin's plea to Joseph is quoted from The Jewish Encyclopedia (1906).

The translations and etymologies of the names of Benjamin's sons draw on Sotah 36b from the Talmud (William Davidson Edition).

The Mary Kim Arnold quotation is from *Litany for the Long Moment*.

Ben Robinson is a poet, musician and librarian. He has only ever lived in Hamilton, Ontario on the traditional territories of the Erie, Neutral, Huron-Wendat, Haudenosaunee and Mississaugas. You can find him online at benrobinson.work.